Cool
Cars

INTRODUCTION

It may be super fast, have a sleek streamlined design, be ultra-modern or incredibly rare, but many different factors come into play to make a car 'cool'. If you see a car in the street and it turns your head making you say "wow, look at that", then it may well be in this book.

There are cars in this i-SPY book that have blistering acceleration or can reach incredibly high speeds. There are also others that are powered by electric engines, while a rare few are both fast and electric. Some cool cars are brand new, while others were originally produced more than 50 years ago. Keep your eyes peeled when you are out and about or head off to a car show and you will spot plenty of cool cars to collect points.

There are some car manufacturers who only make cool cars, but others who are famous for making practical, family cars, every once in a while produce a car which for some reason, is just incredibly cool. There are even cars that start out very uncool but then due to some strange twist of fate – perhaps they are used in a film or TV programme – become genuinely cool.

This i-SPY book has a wide selection of cars that we think are cool for lots of different reasons. There are so many cars around us on the roads today that you will soon see some cool ones.

How to use your i-SPY book

The cars in this book are arranged alphabetically by manufacturer. Points values in circles or stars are shown alongside a picture of the car you need to find, with stars representing harder to spot models. You need 1000 points to send off for your i-SPY certificate (see page 64) but that is not too difficult because there are masses of points in every book. As you make each i-SPY, write your score in the circle or star.

ABARTH FIAT 595

'Hot' versions of the popular Fiat 500. Abarth is the name of a tuning company that has a long association with Fiat and its creations are easy to spot with striking paint and cool scorpion badges. The 595 is quick but the 695 is bonkers – it has only two seats, a roll cage and an engine from a Formula 4 racing car!

Dan Massimiliano / Shutterstock.com

 Points: 40   Top Spot!

AC COBRA

In the 1960s a Texan racing driver called Carroll Shelby created one of the coolest sports cars of all time when he put a Ford V8 engine into a gorgeous but underpowered British sports car called the AC Ace. The 'Cobra' was an instant sensation. You're more likely to spot a replica, but originals, which can fetch more than £1 million, do turn up at car shows and race events.

Martin Lehmann / Shutterstock.com

ALFA ROMEO 4C

Italy's Alfa Romeo has a long and famous tradition of making cars with a sporting edge to them. The 4C is a mid-engined two-seat sports car with a carbon-fibre chassis and a 160mph top speed.

ALFA ROMEO GIULIETTA

Points: 10

Five-door hatchbacks are sensible family cars that are often hard to tell apart. The Giulietta's shield-shaped grille and large wheels mean it stands out. To make it look even sportier, the rear doors are disguised with hidden handles meaning at first glance the car appears to be a two-door.

Points: 10

ALFA ROMEO MITO

In 2008 the MiTo was Alfa Romeo's first ever super-mini. Alfa styling is clear in the big headlights and grille. The name MiTo mixes the Italian cities of 'Milan', where it was designed, and 'Torino' (Turin), where it is made.

Points: 30

The Alfa Romeo 'Duetto' Spider lasted a very long time – 1966 to 1994, through various updates and changes. It always had the same basic two-seat, convertible body and twin-cam engine. The first models had a rounded tail, giving the car's overall shape its Italian nickname: *Osso di sepia*, meaning cuttlefish bone!

 Points: 35

With its inboard suspension, air intake behind the driver's ear and startling lack of bodywork, it looks like a proper open cockpit single-seater racing car. Whether you like or loathe it, you can't help being impressed with the Atom's performance of 0–100mph in six seconds. Quicker than almost any Ferrari…and that's pretty cool.

Points: 30

The letters 'DB' are the initials of David Brown, owner of Aston Martin when a series of classic models were introduced through the 1950s and 60s. The DB5 with its mixture of beautiful Italian design and powerful British engine persuaded the producers of the James Bond films that it would be perfect for 007.

Points: 30

The DB11's biggest boast is an all-new, 5.2-litre V12 engine. The new motor makes far more power – 600bhp, giving a 200mph top speed, thanks to a pair of turbochargers.

Points: 30

Styled like a two-door, the Rapide actually has four making it a rare addition to the Aston family. It will roar up to a 188mph top speed, powered by the 6-litre V12 engine mounted upfront, and it costs about £140,000. Look out for the twin louvres on the bonnet top, to keep that huge engine ventilated.

Points: 30

The Vantage was launched in 2005 to compete head-on against the Porsche 911. It remains the entry level of Aston's range, with numerous special editions and the introduction of a V12-engine spicing things up.

Points: 35

This two-seater sports car is mid-engined, and you can see the air intakes for its V8 or V10 power unit just behind the doors – they're emphasised with a panel painted black in contrast to the rest of the body. Through the rear window the engine is on display, and some R8s have engine bay lighting to show it off at night! Top speed for the V10 is 197mph.

Points: 10

The smooth lines, with no obvious bumpers, of the original 1998 Audi TT were inspired by German Bauhaus architecture and speed record cars of the 1950s. The second-generation TT arrived in 2006 – it's longer, wider and comes with a diesel option. TTs come as 2+2 coupés or two-seater roadsters; score for any you see.

Paulo M. F. Pires / Shutterstock.com

Not many cars get the credit for changing an entire sport, but the Audi Quattro does. Its name refers to its four-wheel drive system and after the Quattro won its second World Rally Championship in 1984, no two-wheel drive car ever won the championship again. What's more, it influenced other car makers to offer 4WD systems on road-going performance cars. After the Quattro, even sporting icons like the Porsche 911 and Lamborghini Diablo were eventually offered with 4WD, and family cars from Alfa Romeo to Toyota started to offer four-wheel traction in all weathers. Many other 4WD Audi models use the Quattro name to this day, but we need you to spot the ice-cool original.

BENTLEY CONTINENTAL GT

First introduced in 2003 it has many stand-out details, like the four separate headlights, mesh grille and old-fashioned bodywork lines of classic Bentleys. This car holds the unusual world speed record for driving on ice, at 205mph!

⭐ **Points: 35** 35

BENTLEY MULSANNE

Named after the long straight at Le Mans, each of these luxury limousines takes 15 weeks to build at Bentley's Cheshire factory. The engine is a 6.75-litre V8. Look for the large mesh grille, big round headlights, and sculpted front wings. Plus, it's over 5.5m long!

BENTLEY BENTAYGA

Points: 25 25

Bentley joined the prestige 4x4 trend when it introduced the Bentayga in 2015. It mixes an extremely luxurious interior with genuine off-road ability and a massively powerful 6-litre engine. At more than £160,000, you'll have to work to spot one.

Points: 20

BMW M6 GRAN COUPÉ

With so many cool BMW 'M cars' to choose from, let's pick the most expensive. The M6 Gran Coupé is not a coupé for your Gran, it's a four-door version of the M6 coupé. It's actually based on the M5 saloon, but is lower, more luxurious and incredibly quick.

BMW i8

Points: 35

A plug-in hybrid supercar? BMW have proved that it's possible. The i8 was unveiled in 2013 with a 1.5-litre, three-cylinder turbocharged petrol motor making 228bhp and a 129bhp electric motor. Use them both at once and 0-60mph takes just 4.5 seconds!

Points: 20

BMW i3

If the i8 is BMW's hybrid flagship model, the i3 is the pure electric option aimed at turning those who might buy a sporty hatchback away from petrol or diesel engines. But while the technology is cool, those futuristic looks are cooler still.

It takes only 20 seconds to raise or lower the concealed metal hardtop of the current Z4, a two-seater sports car. Like all BMWs, it has a grille that some people liken to a pair of kidneys, and in the Z4's case they are flatter and wider than almost any BMW before it. Look out for the BMW badges on front, back and sides.

Points: 30

The first BMW M3, the E30 model, arrived in 1985 and set the standard for all the subsequent M3s to live up to. It's become a cult car, thanks to its aggressive looks, race-tuned engine and excellent handling. Tell it apart from any other old 3-series by the large spoiler and bulging wheel arches.

Points: 30

Bristol started making luxurious, sporting and un-flashy cars for the gentleman enthusiast back in the 1940s and continue to this day. Since 1960 the formula has stayed more or less the same – roomy, two-door body with an American V8 engine, automatic gearbox and a leather-and-wood interior. The Blenheim was the version that lasted into the 21st century.

BUGATTI VEYRON

Top Spot! **Points: 50**

The 'Super Sport' version with its 1200bhp of engine power, can hit 267mph making the Veyron the fastest road-legal production car in the world. It has a horse-shoe-shaped front grille dropping almost to ground level and a curved and bulky rear end in which the 8-litre W16 engine, (16 cylinder) lives. Between 2004–2015 Bugatti built only 450 Veyrons meaning they are incredibly hard to spot. In 2016 it was superseded by the Chiron which is potentially even faster.

CADILLAC COUPE DE VILLE

When you ask someone to think of a classic American car, this is probably what comes to mind! Cadillac made the most of the fins 'n' chrome era with their outrageous 1959 models, and of those the Coupe de Ville is the ultimate cool cruiser. It was powered by an effortless 6.4-litre V8 engine and was nearly six metres long. Score the points for any fin-laden Cadillac.

Points: 30

CATERHAM SUPER SEVEN

This two-seater sports car has often been described as a 'four-wheeled motorbike' because of its exciting driving responses, and also because it's stripped down to the very basics. It has separate mudguards for each wheel, standalone headlights, no boot, a tiny windscreen and a snug cockpit with a tight hood. Beware of look-alikes: only a Caterham will have a big '7' across its front grille.

CHEVROLET CAMARO

The Camaro name became famous in the 1960s when Chevrolet launched a rival to Ford's Mustang. It's still going strong, nowadays in the form of a retro-inspired muscle car in both two-door coupé and convertible forms. The 2016 version could be ordered with a V8 engine or a more efficient turbocharged four-cylinder.

CHEVROLET CORVETTE

Points: 30

Seven versions of 'America's sports car' have been on the market since 1955 and the latest C7 is the fastest yet. The third generation (pictured) however, is the one everyone remembers from the popular road movies of the 1970s. Score for any Corvette you see.

15 **Points: 15**

CHRYSLER 300C

The 300C is unmistakable thanks to its brutal, squared-off looks. It's been around since 2003 but apart from one major redesign in 2011 it's offered the same mixture of road presence and powerful engines ever since. Keep an eye out for the 300C Touring (2003–2010), one of the only cool estate cars you're likely to spot.

The famous little Citroën's name comes from its original taxation class – two horsepower, or *Deux Chevaux*. It had other nicknames, like 'tin snail' and 'umbrella on wheels' but the car's low weight, tiny engine and incredibly supple suspension were needed in rural France and proved popular further afield too.

Staca_5 / Shutterstock.com

CITROËN C4 CACTUS

Citroën are still making wacky cars today. The C4 Cactus with its 'rubber panelled' doors has been showered with praise since it was launched in 2014. Not really a SUV or a hatchback, it's a fun little Citroën that dares to be different, like the best Citroëns of days gone by.

Philip Lange / Shutterstock.com

CITROËN DS

The DS was as revolutionary for large saloons as the 2CV was for lightweight economy cars. A revolutionary suspension system gave a ride so smooth that nothing else came close. Even Rolls-Royce licensed a version of it for their cars. The name? Say 'DS' in a French accent and it sounds like 'Déesse', the French for 'goddess'.

Riley from Christchurch – CC BY 2.0

DELOREAN DMC-12

Jeremy from Sydney CC BY 2.0

For a car that was only in production for 2 years, the Delorean DMC-12 remains one of the most iconic cars of the late 20th century, largely due to its gullwing doors and starring role in the *Back to the Future* films. Unpainted stainless steel body panels textured with a wire brush gave every car the same silvery sheen.

DODGE CHARGER

Points: 30

Philip Lange / Shutterstock.com

The 1968–70 model starred in one of the greatest car chases in movie history – being pursued by the super-cool Steve McQueen in *Bullitt* – before going on to be a lead character in *The Dukes of Hazard*. With 7-litre engines, Chargers had the power to back up the looks!

 Points: 30

DODGE CHALLENGER

Barry Blackburn / Shutterstock.com

Here's Dodge's modern two-door muscle car, competing head to head with the Chevrolet Camaro and Ford Mustang, just like it did in 1970. There are a range of engines available including the Challenger SRT Hellcat that spits out a staggering 707bhp.

FERRARI 488 GTB

Points: 30

The latest mid-engined V8 from Ferrari arrived in 2015 and was immediately declared the greatest driver's car of the year by various magazine road-testers. The performance figures are hard to take in: 0-60mph takes 3.0 seconds, 0–125mph takes 8.3 seconds and the top speed is more than 205mph.

Nadezda Murmakova / Shutterstock.com

Points: 35

FERRARI F12 BERLINETTA

The F12 is the car that has to live up to the tradition of Ferrari's great front-engined, V12-powered, two-seater GTs like the Daytona. It was launched in 2012 to replace the 599 series and despite its greater weight and size, its incredible 730bhp 6.3-litre engine allows it to record very similar performance figures to the 488 GTB.

VanderWolf Images / Shutterstock.com

FERRARI LAFERRARI

Top Spot! **Points: 45**

Every so often Ferrari launches a limited production hypercar. The turn of this century saw the Enzo followed by the FXX and then in 2013 came the LaFerrari. It's actually a revolutionary hybrid that does 0–125mph in less than 7 seconds!

PlusONE / Shutterstock.com

A combination of stunning, shark-nosed beauty and a memorable nickname (better than 365 GTB/4, it's official title!) has ensured that the Daytona is known as one of the coolest, most famous Ferraris of all time. It's the ultimate front-engined Grand Tourer, with just two seats for the lucky occupants, enough room in the boot for weekend luggage and a 4.4-litre V12 engine in the front.

FIAT 124 SPIDER

This car takes the name of a very popular Fiat roadster first made in the 1960s, but it's all new. It actually shares its platform chassis with the Mazda MX5, but the styling and interior give it a character all its own. With a flexible 1.4-litre turbocharged petrol engine and enough comfort for long driving holidays, it looks certain to repeat the success of the original 124 Spider.

Points: 20

FIAT PANDA 100HP

The Panda 100hp is a throwback to the early days of the hot-hatch: a simple, lightweight and affordable car with just enough power to make it fun. For most performance cars 100bhp is nothing these days, but in the little Fiat it was teamed with a six-speed gearbox and proved a perfect mix of pep and economy. Sadly, the model was phased out in 2010 due to emissions regulations, but it's still possible to spot them.

Points: 30

One of the coolest cars of the 1970s was looking a little 'old hat' by the mid-1980s and was phased out, but it's come storming back into fashion recently as a classic symbol of sporty, affordable motoring. It's no longer so affordable though…the most sought-after Capris can change hands for £50,000 or more!

Points: 15

To fans of British Fords, the letters 'RS' mean high performance, good handling and exciting looks. The latest Focus RS offers a mix of 345bhp and four-wheel drive to deliver staggering performance in a £30,000 car: 0-60mph in 4.7 seconds; top speed of 165mph.

Points: 45   Top Spot!

Many car makers have created modern versions of famous older models but none of them is as exciting as Ford's GT. It's the second stab at updating the company's 1960s Le Mans winner, the GT40, and this time a carbon-fibre chassis, compact 3.5-litre, 600bhp V6 and stunning shape set it apart.

Teddy Leung / Shutterstock.com

Ford has been making Mustangs continuously since 1964 but in 2015, for the first time, they were sold in the UK with right-hand drive. The new Mustang harks back to previous models for its aggressive looks, but offers a surprisingly economical four-cylinder turbocharged engine as well as the traditional V8. In either coupé or convertible form, it's the coolest Mustang since the 1960s originals.

Points: 20

HONDA CIVIC TYPE R

The new Civic Type R is a 306bhp monster of a hot hatch with a turbocharged engine and a traditional six-speed manual gearbox. You can spot all Type Rs by the huge rear spoiler and the bold red background to Honda's 'H' badge on the front grille.

HONDA CR-Z

Points: 25

This very small hybrid coupé is unmissable on the road, thanks to its dramatic styling – viewed from the side, the swooping panels seem to present a big metal 'Z' in shape. It has a large snout with the number plate right in the middle of the grille.

Points: 50   **Top Spot!**

HONDA NSX

Honda launched an all-new hybrid-powered NSX at the Chicago Auto Show in 2015 with the first UK deliveries arriving in 2017. At £130,000 there won't be many to spot, but the car makes an intriguing alternative to Ferrari, McLaren, Lamborghini and Porsche models at a similar price. The original NSX was a reliable supercar made between 1990 and 2005.

Points: 20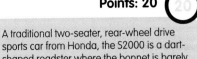

A traditional two-seater, rear-wheel drive sports car from Honda, the S2000 is a dart-shaped roadster where the bonnet is barely higher than the tops of the front wheels, and the headlamps look like narrowed eyes! If you see one with the hood down then you'll notice the twin steel hoops behind the front seats for roll protection.

 Points: 35

This 4x4 off-roader is big, boxy and looks super-tough. It has square wheel arches to accommodate its huge wheels, and a massive, chrome-effect grille at the front with the word H-U-M-M-E-R spelt out across the top. There is a step below the doors to help you climb up into its cabin. Made only between 2005 and 2008, there are a handful in the UK, where it was sold with right-hand drive.

Points: 10

When this four-seater was sold in the UK between 2003 and 2008, it was the coolest car yet from South Korean manufacturer Hyundai as it looked like a small version of the Ferrari 456GT. It has big headlight openings but a tiny front air intake, and some models have a neat air dam at the back.

23

Points: 25

When Enzo Ferrari describes something as 'the most beautiful car in the world' it must be special. From its first appearance in 1961 the E-type was the coolest car on the road. In 1971 it changed from a straight six to a V12 engine and became more of a fast tourer than a sports car, but all of them are worshipped by classic car fans today.

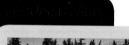

Points: 20

The first Jaguar SUV arrived in 2016, which startled some traditionalists – a diesel 4x4 with a Jaguar badge? However, the car received rave reviews and is proving a hit. The F-Pace is surprisingly capable off road too, but not so much to threaten its sister marque, Land Rover.

Points: 15

The F-type is probably the most well-received sporting Jaguar since the E-type. It replaced the XK in 2014 and its fabulous looks and performance made it a credible, exciting rival to the Porsche 911. Score the same points for the coupé and convertible versions.

Points: 25

This is the car that created Jaguar's reputation for really fast, exciting sports saloon cars. It might not look all that exciting, but you could order one with the same 3.8-litre engine as the E-type, and then there was hardly a four-door car in the world that could keep up. It's a common sight at classic car shows but rare on the road, though you might see one on TV if you find a repeat of *Inspector Morse!*

Points: 10

You'll often see this big, impressive Jaguar model on TV, as the Prime Minister uses one for visits around the country. It has a large simple front grille, a high waistline, a very large high boot and rear light clusters rising up along the tops of the rear wings. The passenger compartment is kitted out like a top-class hotel, and even with a 3-litre diesel engine, performance is impressive – 155mph top speed, 0-60mph in 6.4sec.

Karimyshov / Shutterstock.com

Points: 15

Rob King – CC BY-SA 2.0

When most people think of a Jeep, it's the military-inspired Wrangler that comes to mind, with its separate mudguards front and back, round headlights either side of a row of vertical air intakes and the familiar 'Jeep' name sitting above it. Big fat wheels hint at its four-wheel drive abilities on rough terrain.

Top Spot! Points: 40

Ciari Massimiliano / Shutterstock.com

This incredible supercar, which costs a quarter of a million pounds, can reach 217mph. Gigantic scoops on each side of its carbon fibre body feed air to the 6.5-litre V12 engine in the middle of the car. Sprinting to 60mph from standstill takes just 2.8sec.

Points: 35

Teddy Leung / Shutterstock.com

The Huracan is the replacement for the Gallardo, the smaller of Lamborghini's mid-engined supercars. Thanks to a 5.2-litre V10 and superb handling it can actually out-pace the mighty Aventador on twisty tracks. Cool fact: Lamborghini have built a few for the Italian police!

Sergey Kohl / Shutterstock.com

The Countach is old now – It was made between 1974 and 1990 – but it must be the coolest supercar of all time. Those scissor-lift doors, that crazy geometric shape and the promise of terrifying performance from the howling V12 engine set the bar for all supercars that came afterwards. The name, Countach, is a northern Italian slang word that means something like 'Wow!' or 'Blimey!', which is just about perfect for this car, isn't it?

The idea of building a stubby, mid-engined two-seater and powering it with a Ferrari V6 engine is exciting enough, but Lancia chose this car – originally a design concept from Bertone – to be their main weapon for the World Rally Championship. The car's short wheelbase and low weight (900kg) made it agile and the power from the Ferrari engine provided the speed. The Stratos won the 1974, '75 and '76 championship titles. Only around 500 cars were ever built so finding one on the road in the UK is very rare indeed although they do sometimes turn up at car shows, where they are always very popular exhibits.

The Defender is the final version of the original Land Rover, the British off-road icon inspired by the American army jeep of WW2. The Land Rover was in production from 1948 until 2016 with various revisions and the arrival of larger, more powerful diesel and petrol engines, but considering how long it lasted it's remarkable how little it changed. It became a feature of British life in all sorts of roles, from farm vehicle to stylish urban SUV, but always with the same impressive off-road ability and rugged, basic feel. A replacement is planned for launch in 2019.

 Points: 35

Max Earey / Shutterstock.com

If you associate Lexus with large saloons that fill the luxury market for Toyota, think again. The LFA was a remarkable project that took many years to develop and finally produced 500 production cars between 2010 and 2012. It has a carbon-fibre polymer body and a 4.8-litre V10 engine that revs to 9000rpm and makes an unforgettable, high-pitched scream like a Formula 1 car.

Points: 15

Lotus's neat little sports car is like a Ferrari or Lamborghini in miniature, with side air intakes to cool the mid-mounted engine – which is a 1.6 or 1.8-litre four cylinder unit made by Toyota – and thin, flat headlight units lying on top of the short bonnet. Like the bigger mid-engined sports cars, the Elise is very low to the ground. With the roof in place, the side windows are extremely narrow; once it's removed, it's wind-in-your-hair time!

Points: 25 25

Like many great racing and sports cars, the Evora is mid-engined – and has fantastic road-holding because it's well balanced – but there are two seats in the back for small children. The twin black grilles on the bonnet take air into the cockpit, while at the back it has a spoiler designed in, rather than bolted on, to help the airflow press the car down on to the road.

This Lotus was on sale between 1976 and 2004 in various forms, and has starred in several movies, including the 1977 James Bond film *The Spy Who Loved Me*, in which an Esprit becomes a submarine. One of a series of cars from the late 70s and early 80s with very angular sharp points instead of curving lines it has a long, shark-like, overhung front section with concealed headlights that pop up when switched on. You'll not see many of the older Esprits on the road these days, but when they turn up at shows they still turn heads. Score for any version, classic 'Bond' era or turn of the century models with rounded off corners.

A long, low and curvaceous two-door, four-seater GT car from Italy, its name says it all; *gran turismo* is Italian for 'grand touring', which is exactly what this machine is designed for – fast trips over long distances, travelling in great luxury. The lines of the car curve in and out from front to back, with a prominent, low-down 'snout' at the front and hugely flared openings for the alloy wheels. The V8 engine makes an exciting growling noise as it accelerates 0–60 in 4.7 seconds and keeps going up to a top speed of 187mph.

This Italian-made sports saloon is big and handsome on the outside and you can easily tell it's a Maserati from the chrome 'trident' emblems on its radiator grille and on the roof pillars behind the side windows. Have a look inside if you get the chance – the cabin of the Quattroporte (the word means 'four-door' in Italian) is beautifully trimmed in leather – and try to hear the exciting bark from its V8 engine.

Art Konovalov / Shutterstock.com

25 **Points: 25**

Teddy Leung / Shutterstock.com

The Ghibli borrows its name from a classic Maserati of the past, but that was a long, low two-door GT. The Ghibli is basically a shorter, more compact Quattroporte but with more exciting styling and a more sporting driving experience. It has the choice of various V6 petrol engines, two or four-wheel drive and (believe it or not!) a diesel engine. An economical, sensible Maserati? Perhaps, but it can still touch 150mph.

This MX-5 is the latest version of Mazda's rear-wheel drive two-seater – the third generation of the world's best-selling sports car. It is available with either a traditional fabric roof, that has to be folded by hand, or an electrically operated folding metal hardtop. Headlights are small and thin and there is a bulge right in the middle of the bonnet top. Score for any MX-5 that you see.

Points: 20

20

There's some hidden magic to this four-seater GT car; when the front doors are opened, two small rear doors are revealed and can be opened too, making access to the back seats really easy. Production stopped in 2012, which makes it (for now) the last production car with a rotary engine. It has twin revolving rotors rather than pistons, providing smooth delivery of power…but heavy fuel consumption.

Foto by M / Shutterstock.com

McLaren is a name we know from Formula 1 racing but its road cars are gaining ground against famous names like Ferrari and Porsche. The 'Sports Series' includes the supposedly more affordable (£126,000!) 540C and 570S while the 'Super Series' includes the 650S in Spider and Coupé form and offers even more power and performance. All are mid-engine and make use of F1 construction techniques and high-efficiency turbocharged V8 engines to give acceleration of 0–60mph in just over 3 seconds and top speeds of over 200mph.

This famous car was one of the most daring designs of the twentieth century. It was developed from a powerful six-cylinder racing car but it was the bodywork rather than the impressive performance that set it apart. The doors, as the name suggests, opened upwards like wings in a way the world had never seen before on a production car. Today it's a hugely valuable classic but back in the late 1950s, it was the coolest supercar you could buy.

This stunning two-door coupé has a smooth and slippery shape with a noticeably rounded tail. It's been created by the sports-tuning division of Mercedes to take on the Porsche 911, and with a 4-litre twin-turbo V8 engine and 0-60mph in 3 seconds dead, it looks well capable!

Points: 35

Brabus is an independent tuning house that sells upgraded, customised versions of standard Mercedes models, often with vastly increased performance. There are many, but we've picked the incredible Rocket 900…an S-class limousine with 900bhp!

This is probably the coolest and most unusual estate car on the road today. Its graceful and flowing lines, such as the gentle, tapering curve made by the side window shape, are miles away from the usual 'two-box' profile estate cars possess. It's still very roomy inside for both people and luggage. With the AMG-tuned 5.6-litre V8 engine behind that broad horizontal grille, it's an extremely rapid car.

Points: 15 15

This off-road vehicle looks like it was designed using a ruler! Then again, it was first seen in the 1970s as a high-quality workhorse for extreme terrain like mud, snow and rocks, in the days when most people drove a 4x4 vehicle on the road only to tow a horsebox. The indicators are in little pods on top of the front wings. The most expensive version with a V8 engine costs almost £125,000, so it is less likely to be used by farmers these days.

MERCEDES-BENZ
McLAREN

Top Spot! **Points: 40**

VICTOR TORRES / Shutterstock.com

This extraordinary machine showed us a new type of supercar. It had staggering 200mph performance from its 600bhp supercharged engine and its mid range acceleration during testing was up with the fastest of any production car ever, but it used an automatic gearbox and was easy and comfortable to drive. Spot one by its stretched-out nose and slashes in the front wings.

The MG name is now owned by a Chinese company, though the cars were assembled in Birmingham until 2016. Look for the MG badge on this stylish hatchback, which is sometimes seen with the roof painted a different colour from the body. Different from the old MGs but still a good-looking, nippy little car.

Originally on sale between 1962 and 1981, there are still many of these sports cars, in open roadster and fastback GT form, on Britain's roads. This is because you can still get all the parts to keep them going and there is a large owner's club, but also because owners love driving them. They are old-fashioned cars, with no electronic gadgets, but they're fun to drive and very simple to maintain.

Points: 10

The original Mini is only 3 metres long and is an extremely compact car for four people. It handles like a go-kart with a cheeky character, round headlights, chubby body shape and rain gutters running around the edge of the roof. Over 5 million were built between 1959 and 2001, making it the best-selling British car ever.

Points: 5

When the new Mini arrived in 2001 it was criticized for being so much larger than the original. Now onto its third generation, it's larger than ever, but the Cooper and Cooper S versions are still fun to drive. There's no doubt the car's cheeky image – which is borrowed from the original – helps too!

Points: 15

The 'Evo' started as a dull Japanese saloon but a career in the World Rally Championship allowed Mitsubishi to develop it into one of the most exciting four-doors cars of the last 20 years. Each new generation has kept the same formula: a two-litre, turbocharged engine, four-wheel drive and a lot of aggressive-looking scoops and spoilers!

An unusual British sports car that mixes high technology with tradition. It has flowing separate mudguards with its big headlights smoothed into the front either side of a 'waterfall' grille. The roof has detachable aluminium panels that can be stored in the boot. The cockpit is narrow and snug, and the handmade car is powered by a BMW V8 engine.

Points: 20

Morgan celebrated its 100th anniversary in 2010; it's the oldest car manufacturer still owned by the founder's family. The hand-built cars still have a separate chassis, with body frame made of seasoned ash timber, although the engine is the very latest Ford V6 or four cylinder. Owners enjoy 'vintage' motoring with modern reliability.

⭐ **Points: 35**

Morgan amazed the car world by returning to three-wheelers in 2011 after a gap of 59 years; it was immediately overwhelmed with orders for the car, which has its single wheel at the back. Its twin-cylinder engine, which is a huge 1983cc in capacity, is completely exposed at the front, while the body, with its open cockpit, tapers to a point at the back.

NISSAN 370Z

Darren Brode / Shutterstock.com

Unlike most other Nissans you can buy in the UK, the 370Z has drive going to the rear wheels only. Combined with the 326bhp of power from its 3.7-litre V6 engine at the front, this makes for a true sports car driving experience. The 370Z has the much-loved long bonnet/short rear end look, with the bodywork bulging dramatically around the wheels, and a seemingly tiny cabin with a low roofline.

Points: 30

NISSAN FIGARO

Kagai19927 / Shutterstock.com

Although this car looks like it has driven straight out of the 1950s, with its chrome details, painted wheel discs and roll-back convertible roof, it was built in 1991 as a limited edition of 20,000. They are usually two-tone, with a white roof above a pastel-coloured body. It's very easy and economical to drive because, under those retro clothes, the Figaro is identical to an automatic Nissan Micra, and owners love them.

Teddy Leung / Shutterstock.com

The GT-R seems to have bodywork rippling with muscles and indeed this big two-door, four-seater coupé provides a formidable performance from its 3.8-litre V6 engine, tuned like a racing car's to give 550bhp. In fact, the whole car has been developed from competition cars and the GT-R will reach a 193mph top speed. The chunky front end appears to leap forward, while at the back a tail spoiler on the huge boot sits above four circular rear lights.

PEUGEOT 205 GTi

If the VW Golf GTi made hot hatchbacks a success, Peugeot's little 205 GTi made them fun. They came in 1.6 and 1.9 litre versions (you can tell which by looking at the badge by the rear side window) but both of them were light, quick and exciting to drive.

15 **Points: 15**

PEUGEOT 207 CC

The open version of the big-selling 207 came with an ingenious folding metal hardtop that makes it a true coupé convertible – hence the CC name. The windscreen is steeply raked right over the two front seats, enabling the short roof section to connect up with it. Peugeot's lion badge is framed in a large four-sided section on the nose.

PEUGEOT RCZ

This aggressive, low-to-the-ground coupé is the sportiest Peugeot ever, making it a rival to cars like the Audi TT. The low body shape is full of big curves, with the rear portion of the car looking quite self-contained. Two bright metal sections taper up and over the side windows, sandwiching the glass roof. The twin rear exhaust pipes are offset to the left.

The very first Porsches were little more than tuned VW Beetles with streamlined bodies, but they evolved fast. In 1963, when the 911 was launched, they made their biggest leap by changing up from four-cylinders to six, giving much more power and potential. The format of a rear-mounted, air-cooled engine in a tapering two-door body was so successful that it stayed pretty much the same until a water-cooled version arrived in 1998!

Points: 30

The Turbo has been a thrilling high-powered variant of the 911 since the first one appeared in 1975. You can usually spot them by their large rear spoilers, wider 'hips' and air intakes to help cool the engine. The latest version has up to 560bhp in the Turbo S model with a 0-60mph time of 2.9 seconds! From late 2015, even the base model 911 started using a turbocharged engine.

This Porsche sports car is more affordable than the 911, and is a mid-engined two-seater, which explains the subtle air intakes just behind the doors. The styling is simple and graceful, and the rear spoiler only reveals itself (it cuts across the rear lights) by rising when the Boxster accelerates past 75mph. Older Boxsters look fairly similar – score for any you see.

Points: 25

As the 911 became faster, more luxurious and more expensive, Porsche launched more affordable entry level sports cars with the Boxter in 1996 and the Cayman in 2005. The Cayman's performance and handling actually mirrors that of the early 911s. Tell it from its more expensive sibling by its stubbier back end and kicked-up side window line.

Points: 25

Most luxury saloons are upright and formal-looking, but this big, expensive four-door Porsche is flat and broad with coupé-like side windows and a large flat rear screen. The Panamera has its engine at the front with both two- and four-wheel drive options and unlike other large luxury cars, the Panamera has a hatchback fifth door.

Points: 15

The very first Range Rover arrived in 1970, and for the next 26 years barely changed at all, which is why this legendary off-roader came to be known as the Classic. It stands tall and has deep windows all round, with the bonnet forming the top part of the wings. In contrast to the severe angular styling, the headlights are always round.

Points: 5

From its slim cheese-grater grille at the front to its narrow rear screen and 'short' windows the Evoque stands out. The slanted waistline and wide wheel arches make its alloy wheels and tyres look huge. This British-made 4x4 has been a runaway success as the most compact Range Rover ever, and the car is unusual in being available as a two-door coupé and a five-door estate. Try and get a peek at the stylish dashboard.

This seems like a contradiction in terms – a sporty Range Rover? But it's become a highly successful model, combining a slightly lower, more compact body with a powerful range of engines (and an optional hybrid powertrain) on a well-developed chassis. It really does drive like a sports car on stilts, but you have to pay for the privilege: the fastest SVR version costs more than £100,000.

Points: 20

This is Renault's sporty version of their best-selling Megane hatchback. The RS stands for Renault Sport, Renault's motorsport division, and many different versions have been offered since the first one in 2004. They have turbocharged engines, a lower ride height than normal Meganes, big alloy wheels and jazzy interiors with sports seats. They're seen as some of the best hot hatchbacks of recent years.

Points: 35

This nifty roadster was never a common sight – only 100 were made in right-hand drive, though you may see one of the European versions or even one of the racing cars. The Spider was created both as a road car and racing car for its own one-make race series. Although a terrific little sports car it was too far from Renault's every-day range to remain in production for long.

Points: 35

So many things about this city car are unique on British roads today. Obviously, the body is a pod with the wheels jutting out at each corner. There are no doors as standard (they are optional) but hinged side impact bars. The seating is for two people in tandem and it is entirely electric, recharged at the mains. Great for the city.

The Phantom is one of the all-round biggest cars available – it's a huge, impressive limousine favoured by millionaires, royalty and celebrities. Its front grille looks like a model of a Greek temple, and the famous 'Spirit of Ecstasy' flying lady mascot stands proud above it. Headlights are rectangles. The rear end of the car, in contrast, is graceful and soft-edged. Look at the wheels and see how the Rolls-Royce emblems stay upright at all times. This is a truly impressively large car when seen on the road although due to their exclusivity they are pretty hard to spot.

Points: 40   **Top Spot!**

Teddy Leung / Shutterstock.com

For a quarter of a million pounds, you can buy the most luxurious two-door coupé on the market. Rolls-Royce introduced the Wraith in 2013 to join a line-up that includes the Dawn (a closely related convertible) and the Ghost (a longer four-door version) as well as the Phantom (previous page). As with the rest of the RR range, the Wraith is more than utter comfort and elegance as its performance is close to that of some of the sportier entries in this book. It offers 0–60mph acceleration in just over 4 seconds and a top speed of well over 150mph. You couldn't mix it up with another car, but to be certain, check for those incredible doors that hinge at the back!

Saab wasn't the first car maker to produce turbo-charged models (that honour goes to Oldsmobile in America) but it was the Saab Turbo that introduced affordable turbocharging to family cars and started a revolution. The Saab 99 Turbo came first in 1978 with the similar 900 Turbo following on until 1994. Look for the black rubber spoiler across the base of the rear windscreen and front and rear Turbo badges.

This very small sports car was on sale between 2003 and 2006, and shared the turbocharged three-cylinder 0.7-litre engine of the Smart city car. The car is very short and low. The Roadster model has a flat panel over the rear engine, the Roadster Coupé has a glazed, boxed-in back end and both can come with either a removable roof panel or an electrically-operated soft-top.

Points: 15

Are they cool or just way over the top? Your opinion might depend on whether you were riding in one or watching it cruise past! Almost any car can be chopped in half and lengthened by skilful coach-builders, but the most common subjects seem to be American SUVs and Cadillacs, followed by luxury cars such as Mercedes and Jaguars.

Points: 10

Subaru went head to head with Mitsubishi through the 1990s and 2000s in the World Rally Championship, winning three constructor's titles and three driver's titles with the Impreza. The road cars closely related to these competition machines have a huge cult following, with the WRX STI models made from 1992 to 2007 regarded as the classics, though the WRX STI is still offered today. Look out for World Rally Blue paint and gold wheels – common features on WRX 'Scoobies'.

Taina Sohlman / Shutterstock.com

Tesla are busy re-writing the rule book on electric cars. Until the Roadster appeared in 2006, cars driven by batteries were tiny urban runabouts, never sports cars. But the Model S has gone one better by offering blistering sports-car performance in the sleek, handsome body of an executive saloon. Since customer deliveries began in 2012, more than 130,000 have been built and a network of Tesla 'Superchargers' – fast-charging points that give the car an extra 170 miles in 30 minutes – has grown. Keep an eye out for them at motorway service stations. New models are arriving to join the Model S, but the S itself keeps making leaps in power and range. The P100D version, announced in August 2016, should manage more than 300 miles between stops and sprint from 0-60mph in a mind-boggling 2.5 seconds.

TOYOTA GT86

A compact coupé with tight lines and a long bonnet/short boot look, the GT86 has a neat spoiler at the back and twin exhaust pipes exiting the car through a diffuser panel below the boot lid. It's designed to be an old-fashioned fun car to drive, which means drive to the rear wheels, no turbocharger on the 2-litre petrol engine and fairly narrow tyres; the cockpit is simple and the rev-counter is the biggest dial…

Points: 15 **15**

TOYOTA iQ

You'll immediately notice that the iQ is very compact. Lots of thought has gone into freeing up space for the cabin, which means it has thinner seats, a compact air conditioning unit and even a thin, flat fuel tank. The engine is a low polluting three-cylinder. Almost the whole side of the car is taken up with the large door as there is virtually no bonnet or boot!

If the Land Rover is cool, so is Toyota's take on the same thing. Japanese engineering and attention to detail meant that in the toughest, hottest places such as Australia, the Land Cruiser soon outsold all its rivals. There are many shapes and models but you can score for any of them.

Eugene Sergeev / Shutterstock.com

Before the GT86, Toyota made a long line of powerful front-engined coupés called Supras. The first Supra was a sporty version of the Celica but became a model in its own right in 1986. By the 1990s,

it had become a very fast and capable car, with the twin-turbo version offering Porsche 911-beating performance: 177mph top speed and 0-60mph in 4.6 seconds.

GRIFFITH

This desirable TVR from the 1990s seems like a mixture of muscle car and soft-top sports car. It has a thunderous V8 engine and in its most powerful form (the Griffith 500) it can leap from 0-60mph in a fraction over 4 seconds. The name comes from an earlier V8 TVR created in the 1960s when TVR's American importer, Jack Griffith, put a Ford V8 engine into one of the firm's little Grantura GT cars.

SAGARIS

Points: 35 35

The last and perhaps wildest TVR model before the original firm's collapse in 2006 is recognisable for the numerous slashes in the bodywork. They are supposed to help aerodynamics and cooling but they also add to the incredibly cool, almost cartoonish looks of the Sagaris. A relaunched TVR in cooperation with F1 designer Gordon Murray and Cosworth, plan to deliver new models from 2017.

VAUXHALL VX220

The VX220 has a similar size and shape to the Lotus Elise, which isn't too much of a surprise because both cars share the same bonded aluminium chassis. And they were built side by side in the Lotus factory in Norfolk. The Vauxhall, which comes with or without a turbocharger, looks more solid and boxy than the Lotus, with a simple vertical air intake behind the doors for the mid-mounted engine. It has a bright metal windscreen surround and a lift-out roof panel.

Points: 30

VAUXHALL MONARO

Vauxhall is part of General Motors, which in Australia has the Holden brand. 'Monaro' is a name that Holden first used for a sporty coupé back in 1968, but it got a brawny re-launch in 2001 when this sleek coupé arrived with a 5.7-litre V8 borrowed from Chevrolet, another GM division. Vauxhall sold it under their own name from 2004 to 2006 and it became a modest success. Look out for the 6.0-litre VXR version with even more tyre-smoking performance.

25 **Points: 25**

You could call the Beetle the most important car of the 20th century, but apart from its history the companies it created – Volkswagen and Porsche – wouldn't exist today without it. It's the centre of a world-wide scene, with customising, restoration and competition in a thousand forms.

Points: 10

The 'New' Beetle became a common sight on UK roads after its relaunch in 1997, so to make this more of a challenge we want you to find the latest model which came out in 2012. It is longer, wider and with a lower roof line than the Beetle it replaces, with more integrated light clusters at the back and a full-width air intake with more angular corners at the front below bumper level.

20 **Points: 20**

The VW 'camper van' has been around since the 1950s and evolved through many versions, but the original kind with air-cooled engines at the back are still such a common sight that you know what an immense success the Volkswagen Type 2 has been.

Volkswagen have clearly had the knack of making popular models that the public keep buying for years and years as indicated with the Beetle and camper van on the previous page. While those two vehicles took time to become cool, the original Golf GTi was cool from the off. It was introduced in 1976 and although it wasn't technically the first sporty hatchback, its arrival certainly kicked off the Hot Hatch era. 40 years later and the Golf GTi, now in its seventh incarnation, is still a key model for VW. Originals like the one shown here are uber-cool collectors' items, but score for any.

In the 1960's with the P1800 Volvo made a car that was cool as well as reliable. It was made famous by use in the TV series *The Saint* but much more remarkable is the achievement of an American man called Irvin Gordon. He bought his P1800 new in 1966 and as of 2016 has used it to cover more than 3 million miles – a world record!

A folding metal hardtop is the big feature on this four-seater Swedish convertible. Being a very practical car company, Volvo has made sure there is also plenty of room for luggage by designing an extra-long boot. The Volvo badge is derived from the ancient symbol for iron.